Tori Amos Anth

Her life in music.
A compilation of 25 songs from all facets of an extraordinary musical career.

Amsco Publications
New York/London/Sydney

Cover photography by Terry Richardson
Interior photography by the Amos family, Atlantic Records, Alan Friedman, Katerina Jebb
and Martina Hoogland, Cindy Palmano, Rankin, Billy Reckert,
Terry Richardson and Eric Rosse

Order No. AM 947331
US International Standard Book Number: 0.8256.1663.8
UK International Standard Book Number: 0.7119.6291.X

Exclusive Distributors:
Music Sales Corporation
257 Park Avenue South, New York, NY 10010 USA
Music Sales Limited
8/9 Frith Street, London W1V 5TZ England
Music Sales Pty. Limited
120 Rothschild Street, Rosebery, Sydney, NSW 2018, Australia

Printed in the United States of America by
Vicks Lithograph and Printing Corporation

Contents

Baltimore

It's so nice to live here
I'm glad this is my home
I've got a homestead on Baltimore Street
it's someplace to call my own

it's all kinds of people
familiar places smiling faces
I'm proud to say I'm a Baltimorian
but the 'Birds' are the best
the best of Baltimore

we like it here in Baltimore
there's so much love in Baltimore
working hand in hand
to make this place a better land in Baltimore
love is what you'll find so stop and take the time
I've got Oriole baseball on my mind

we like it here in Baltimore
there's so much love in Baltimore
working hand in hand

to make this place a better land in Baltimore
love is what you'll find so stop and take the time
to enjoy the brotherhood of Baltimore

the sun sets across the bay
I'm glad I spend my day
in a working American city
with all the people who make it that way
it's time to jump in a taxi
for Thirty-third Street
knowing I'll be watching those 'Birds' go,
watching Weaver's show

we like it here in Baltimore
there's so much love in Baltimore
we're working hand in hand
to make this place a better land in Baltimore
love is what you'll find so stop and take the time
I've got Oriole baseball on my mind

on my mind in Baltimore

Baltimore

Words and Music by Tori Amos

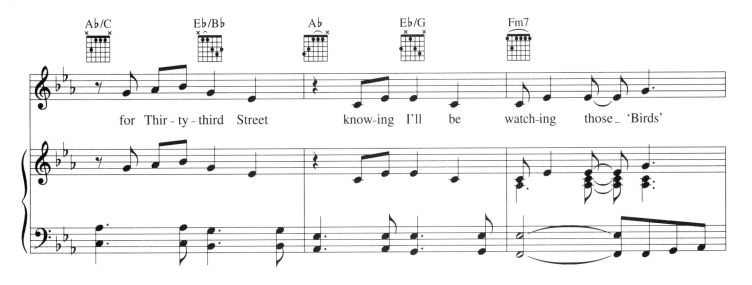

for Thir - ty - third Street   know - ing I'll   be   watch - ing   those _ 'Birds'

go, _____   watch - ing Weav - er's   show _____

D.S. al Coda ⊕

⊕ **Coda**

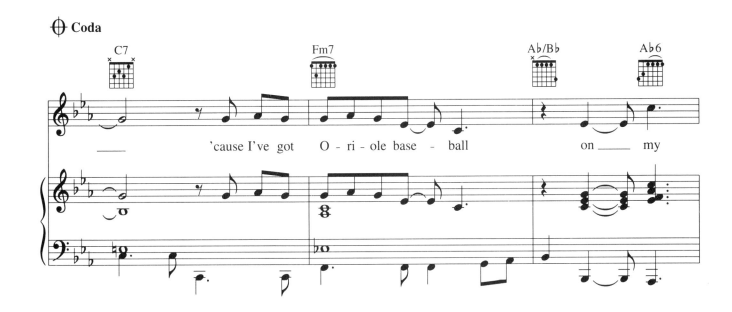

_____   'cause I've got   O - ri - ole base - ball   on ____ my

Rubies and Gold

Rubies and Gold
star of my moonlight
warmer than roses in spring
The kingdoms were sold
to hold their beauty, well
I'd sell my life anyway
just to say I held their heart in my arms
there's strength in my soul

Rubies and Gold
are you to me
You're a jewel upon my chest
warming my heart with your kisses,
a peaceful way to rest
fullfilling my life long wishes

And silently you're watching me
stroking my cheek with your hand
your eyes are deep yet filled with tears
I've never seen so much love in a man.

Rubies and Gold
star of my moonlight
warmer than roses in spring
The kingdoms were sold
to hold their beauty, well
I'd sell my life anyway
just to say I held their heart in my arms
there's strength in my soul

Rubies and Gold
you are to me

Rubies And Gold

Words and Music by Tori Amos and Mike Amos

Ru - bies and Gold   star   of   my   moon— light

Etienne

Maybe I'm a witch lost in time
running through the fields of Scotland by your side
kicked out of France but I still believe
taken to a land far across the sea

Etienne, Etienne
hear the west wind whisper my name
Etienne, Etienne
by the morning maybe we'll remember who I am

maybe you're the knight who saved my life
maybe we faced the fire side by side
here we are again under the same sky
as the gypsy crystal slowly dies

Etienne, Etienne
hear the west wind whisper my name
Etienne, Etienne
by the morning maybe we'll remember who I am

I close my eyes see you again
I know I've held you but I can't remember where or when

Etienne, Etienne
hear the west wind whisper my name
Etienne, Etienne
by the morning maybe we'll remember who I am

maybe I'm a witch

Etienne

Words and Music by Tori Amos

Moderately, in 2

May-be I'm a

1. witch
2. knight

lost in time
who saved my life

run-ning through the
may-be we

Floating City

You went away
why did you leave me
you know I believed you
nothing explained
where are the answers
I know I need you
tell me is your city paved with gold
is there hunger
do your people grow old
do your governments have secrets that they've sold

every night I wait take me away
to your floating city
by my window at night
I see the lights to your floating city
come and take me away
I want to play in your floating city
floating city

T.V. turns off
any of us that
say that we've seen you
tell me are we
the only planet
that can't conceive you
will we be like Atlantis long ago
so assured that we're advanced
with what we know
that our spirit never had time to grow

is it weak to look for
saviors out in space
little Earth she tries so hard
to change our ways
sometimes she must get
sick of this place

Floating City

Words and Music by Tori Amos

Moderately slow, with a strong beat

1. You went _ a - way _ why did you leave
2. *See additional lyrics*
3. *Instrumental*

_ me you know I be - lieved _ you

float - ing cit - y   yeah   float - ing   cit - y

Additional lyrics

2. T.V. turns off
   any of us that
   say that we've seen you
   tell me are we
   the only planet
   that can't conceive you
   will we be like Atlantis long ago
   so assured that we're advanced
   with what we know
   that our spirit never had time to grow

3. is it weak to look for
   saviors out in space
   little Earth she tries so hard
   to change our ways
   sometimes she must get
   sick of this place

Silent All These Years excuse me but can I be you for a while my DOG won't bite if you sit real still I got the anti-Christ in the kitchen yellin' at me again yeah I can hear that been saved again by the garbage truck I got something to say you know but NOTHING comes yes I know what you think of me you never shut-up yeah I can hear that *but what if I'm a mermaid in these jeans of his with her name still on it hey but I don't care cause some-times I said sometimes I hear my voice and its been HERE silent all these years* so you found a girl who thinks really deep thoughts what's so amazing about really deep thoughts boy you best pray that I bleed real soon how's that thought for you my scream got lost in a paper cup you think there's a heaven where some screams have gone I got 25 bucks and a cracker do you think it's enough to get us there years go by will I still be wait-ing for somebody else to understand years go by if I'm stripped of my beauty and the orange clouds raining in my head years go by will I choke on my tears till finally there is nothing left one more casualty you know we're too EASY easy easy well I love the way we communicate your eyes focus on my funny lip shape let's hear what you think of me now but baby don't look up in the sky is falling your MOTHER shows up in a nasty dress it's your turn now to stand where I stand everybody lookin' at you here take hold of my hand yeah I can hear them

Silent All These Years

Words and Music by Tori Amos

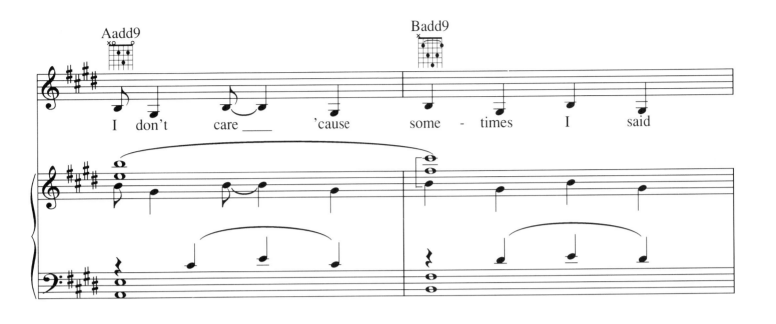

I don't care ____ 'cause some - times I said

Some - times I hear my voice _____ and it's ____ been

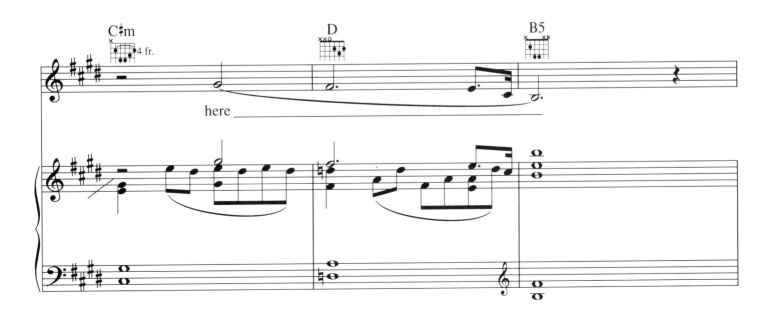

here _____

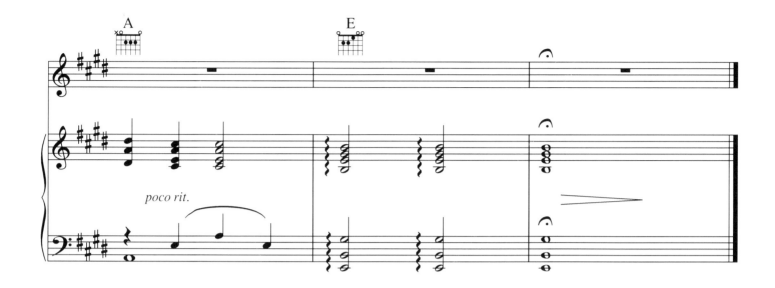

2. So you found a girl who thinks really deep thoughts
   What's so amazing about really deep thoughts
   Boy you best pray that I bleed real soon
   How's that thought for you

   My scream got lost in a paper cup
   You think there's a heaven where some screams have gone
   I got twenty-five bucks and a cracker
   Do you think it's enough...to get us there
   Cause

   (Chorus to 2nd ending)

(𝄋) 3. Well, I love the way we communicate
   Your eyes focus on my funny lip shape
   Let's hear what you think of me now
   But baby don't look up the sky is falling

   Your mother shows up in a nasty dress
   It's your turn now to stand where I stand
   And everybody lookin' at you
   Here take hold of my hand...yeah, I can hear them
   But

   (Chorus to Coda)

Winter snow can wait I forgot my mittens wipe my nose get my new boots on I get a little warm in my heart when I think of winter I put my hand in my father's glove I run off where the DRIFTS GET DEEPER sleeping beauty trips me with a frown I hear a voice "you must learn to stand up for yourself cause I can't always be around" *he says when you gonna make up your mind when you gonna love you as much as I do when you gonna make up your mind cause things are gonna CHANGE so fast all the white horses are still in bed I tell you that I'll always want you near you say that things change my dear* boys get discovered as winter MELTS flowers competing for the sun years go by and I'm here still waiting withering where some snowman was mirror mirror where's the crystal palace but I can only see myself SKATING around the truth who I am but I know dad the ice is getting thin hair is grey and the fires are burning so many dreams on the shelf you say I wanted you to be PROUD of me I always wanted that myself he says when you gonna make up your mind when you gonna love you as much as I do when you gonna make up your mind cause things change so fast all the WHITE HORSES have gone ahead I tell you that I always want you near you say that things change my dear

Winter

Words and Music by Tori Amos

Boys get discovered as winter melts
Flowers competing for the sun
Years go by and I'm here still waiting
Withering where some snowman was.

Mirror mirror where's the crystal palace
But I only can see myself
Skating around the truth who I am
But I know Dad the ice is getting thin.

(Chorus to 2nd ending)

Happy Phantom and if I die today I'll be the HAPPY phantom and I'll go chasin' the nuns out in the yard and I'll run naked through the streets without my mask on and I will never need umbrellas in the rain I'll wake up in strawberry fields every day and the atrocities of school I can forgive the HAPPY phantom has no right to bitch *oo who the time is getting closer oo who time to be a ghost oo who every day we're getting closer the sun is getting dim will we pay for who we been* so if I die today I'll be the HAPPY phantom and I'll go wearin' my NAUGHTIES like a jewel they'll be my ticket to the universal opera there's Judy Garland taking Buddha by the hand and then these seven little men get up to dance they say Confucius does his crossword with a pen I'm still the angel to a girl who hates to SIN or will I see you dear and wish I could come back you found a girl that you could TRULY love again will you still call for me when she falls asleep or do we soon forget the things we cannot see

Happy Phantom

Words and Music by Tori Amos

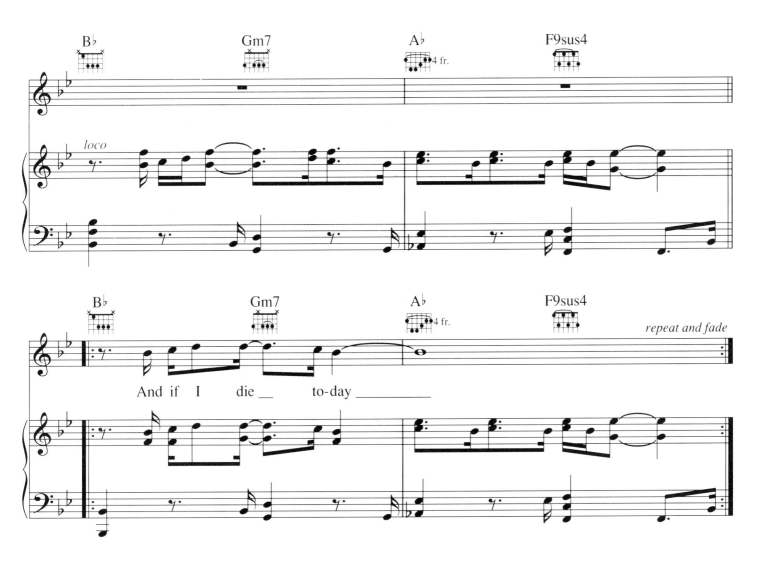

And if I die __ to-day _____

2. So if I die today I'll be a happy phantom
   And I'll go wearin' my naughties like a jewel
   They'll be my ticket to the universal opera
   There's Judy Garland taking Buddha by the hand
   And then these seven little men get up to dance
   They say Confucius does his crossword with a pen
   I'm still the angel to a girl who hates to sin

   (Chorus to 2nd ending)

Mother go go go go now out of the nest it's time to go go go now circus girl without a safety net here here now don't cry you raised your hand for the assignment tuck those ribbons under your helmet be a good soldier first my left foot then my right behind the OTHER pantyhose running in the cold *mother the car is here somebody leave the light on green limousine for the red-head DANCING dancing girl and when I dance for him somebody leave the light on just in case I like the dancing I can remember where I come from* I walked into your dream and now I've forgotten how to dream my own dream you are the CLEVER one aren't you brides in veils for you we told you all of our secrets all but one so don't you even try the phone has been disconnected dripping with blood and with time and with your advice poison me against the MOON I escape into your escape into our very favorite fearscape it's across the sky and I cross my heart and I cross my legs oh my god first my left foot then my right behind the other breadcrumbs lost under the snow

Mother

Words and Music by Tori Amos

Moderate, flowingly (in 2)

1. Go   go ____   go _____   go   now ___

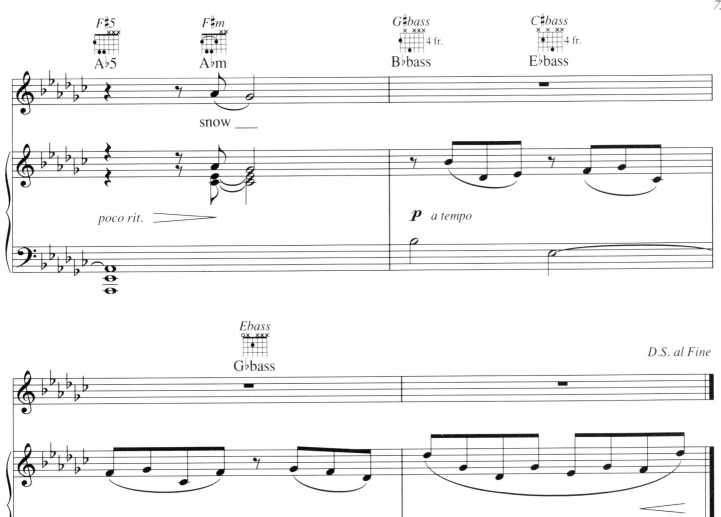

I walked into your dream
And now I've forgotten
How to dream my own dream
You are the clever one aren't you
Brides in veils for you
We told you all of our secrets
All but one so don't you even try
The phone has been disconnected
Dripping with blood and with time
And with your advice
Poison me against the moon

Mother the car is here
Somebody leave the light on
Black chariot for the redhead
Dancing dancing girl
He's gonna change my name
Maybe you'll leave the light on
Just in just in case I like the dancing
I can remember where I come from

(2nd ending to instrumental solo)

Precious Things so I ran faster but it caught me here yes my loyalties turned like my ankle in the seventh grade running after BILLY running after the rain *these precious things let them bleed let them wash away these precious things let them break their hold over me* he said you're really an ugly girl but I like the way you play and I died but I thanked him can you believe that sick holding on to his picture dressing up every day I wanna smash the faces of those beautiful BOYS those christian boys so you can make me cum that doesn't make you Jesus I remember yes in my peach party dress no one dared no one cared to tell me where the pretty girls are those demigods with their NINE-INCH nails and little fascist panties tucked inside the heart of every nice girl

Precious Things

Words and Music by Tori Amos

Mary

Everybody wants something from you
everybody want a piece of Mary
lush valley all dressed in green
just ripe for the picking

god I want to get you out of here
you can ride in a pink Mustang
when I think of what we've done to you
Mary can you hear me

growing up isn't always fun
they tore your dress and stole your ribbons
they see you cry they lick their lips
well butterflies don't belong in nets

Mary can you hear me
Mary you're bleeding, Mary don't be afraid
we're just waking up and I hear help is on the way
Mary can you hear me
Mary, like Jimmy said, Mary don't be afraid
"cause even the wind even the wind cries your name"

everybody wants you sweetheart
everybody got a dream of glory
Las Vegas got a pinup girl
they got her armed as they buy and sell her
rivers of milk running dry
can't you hear the dolphins crying
what'll we do when our babies scream
fill their mouths with some acid rain

Mary can you hear me
Mary you're bleeding, Mary don't be afraid
we're just waking up and I hear help is on the way
Mary can you hear me
Mary, like Jimmy said, Mary don't be afraid
"cause even the wind even the wind cries your name"

Mary

Words and Music by Tori Amos

Slow, steady 4

⊕ Coda

Take To The Sky

This house is like Russia with eyes cold and grey
you got me moving in a circle, I dyed my hair red today

I just want a little passion to hold me in the dark
I know I got some magic buried, buried deep in my heart
but my priest says you ain't saving no souls
my father says you ain't makin' any money
my doctor says you just took it to the limit
and here I stand with this sword in my hand

you can say it one more time what you don't like
let me hear it one more time
then have a seat while I take to the sky

my heart is like the ocean it gets in the way
so close to touching freedom then I hear the guards call my name
and my priest says you ain't saving no souls
my father says you ain't makin' any money
my doctor says you just took it to the limit
and here I stand with this sword in my hand

you can say it one more time what you don't like
let me hear it one more time
then have a seat while I take to the sky

if you don't like me just a little, well, why do you hang around
if you don't like me just a little why do you take it

this house is like Russia
you can say it one more time you can say it one more time
you can say it one more time what you don't like
let me hear it one more time
then have a seat while I take to the sky

Take To The Sky

Words and Music by Tori Amos

Moderately, with a strong beat

Sweet Dreams

"Lie, lie, lies ev'rywhere," said the father to the son
your peppermint breath gonna choke 'em to death
daddy watch your little black sheep run
he got a knives in his back every time he opens up
you say, "he gotta be strong if he wanna be a man"
mister I don't know how you can have

sweet dreams sweet dreams.

land, land of liberty
we're run by a constipated man
when you live in the past
you refuse to see when your
daughter come home nine months pregnant
with five billion points of light
gonna shine em on the face of your friends
they got the earth in a sling
they got the world on her knees
they even got your zipper between their teeth

sweet dreams sweet dreams.

you say you say you say you have em I say that you're a liar
sweet dreams sweet dreams

go on, go on, go on and dream
your house is on fire
come along now

well, well, summer wind been catching up with me
"elephant mind, missy you don't have
you forgettin' to fly,
darlin', when you sleep"
I got a hazy lazy Susan
takin turns all over my dreams
I got lizards and snakes runnin' through my body
funny how they all have my face.

sweet dreams sweet dreams

Sweet Dreams

Words and Music by Tori Amos

1. "Lie,   lie, __ lies   ev-'ry-where," said the   fa - ther to __ the son _____   your
2.,3. (D.S.) See additional lyrics

pep-per-mint breath gon-na choke 'em to death dad-dy watch   your   lit-tle   black sheep run _ he got a

⊕ Coda

Additional lyrics

2. land, land of liberty
   we're run by a constipated man
   when you live in the past
   you refuse to see when your
   daughter come home nine months pregnant
   with five billion points of light
   gonna shine 'em on the face of your friends
   they got the earth in a sling
   they got the world on her knees
   they even got your zipper in between their teeth

3. well, well, summer wind been catching up with me
   "elephant mind, missy you don't have
   you forgettin' to fly,
   darlin', when you sleep"
   I got a hazy lazy Susan
   takin' turns all over my dreams
   I got lizards and snakes runnin' through my body.
   Funny how they all have my face.

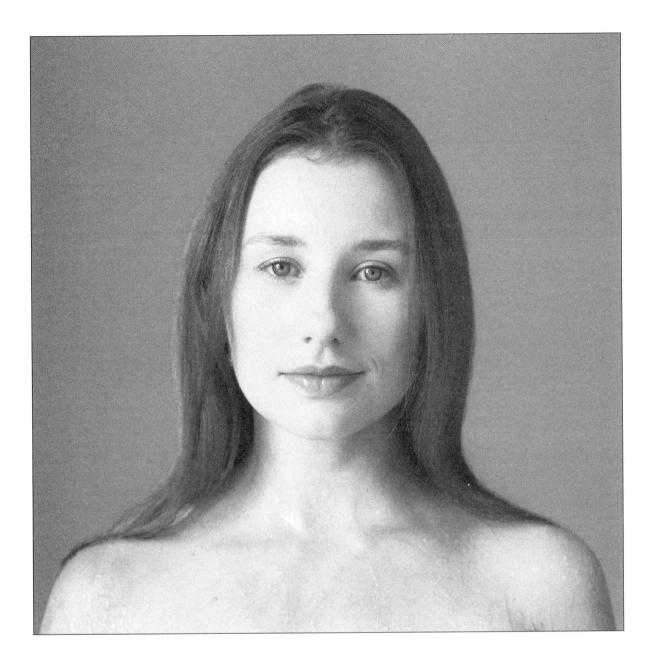

Honey

A little dust never stopped me none he liked my shoes I kept them on
sometimes I can hold my tongue sometimes not,
when you just skip-to-loo my darlin'
and you know what you're doin' so don't even

you're just too used to my honey now
you're just too used to my honey

and I think I could leave your world
if she was the better girl
so when we died I tried to bribe the undertaker
cause I'm not sure what you're doin' or the reasons

you're just too used to my honey now
you're just too used to my honey

don't bother coming down
I made a friend of the western sky
don't bother coming down
you always liked your babies tight

turn back one last time love to watch those cowboys ride
but cowboys know cowgirls ride on the Indian side
and you know what you're doin' so don't even

you're just too used to my honey now
you're just too used to my honey

Honey

Words and Music by Tori Amos

Moderately

with pedal

A lit-tle dust nev-er stopped me none ___ he liked my shoes ___ I kept them on ___

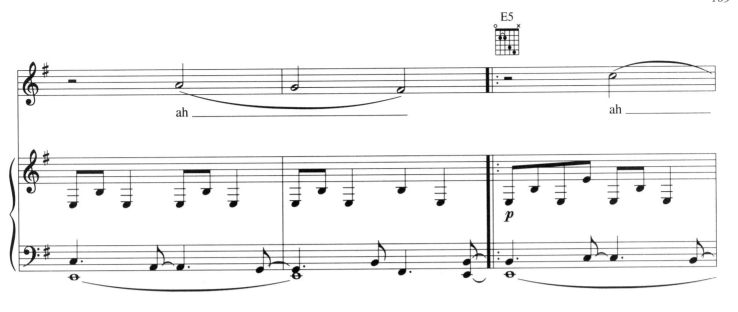

Past the Mission

I don't believe I went too far I said I was willing she said she knew what my books did not I thought she knew what's up

Past the mission behind the prison tower past the mission I once knew a hot girl past the mission they're closing every hour past the mission I smell the roses

She said they all think they know him well she knew him better everyone wanted something from him I did too but I shut my mouth he just gave me a smile

Hey they found a body not sure it was his but they're using his name and she gave him shelter and somewhere I know she knows somethings only she knows

Past The Mission

Words and Music by Tori Amos

Space Dog

Way to go Mr. Microphone show us all what you don't know centuries secret societies he's our commander still space dog

so sure we were on something your feet are finally on the ground he said so sure we were on something your feet are just on the ground girl

rain and snow our engines have been receiving your eager call there's Colonel Dirtyfishydishcloth he'll distract her good don't worry so

and to the one you thought was on your side she can't understand she truly believes the lie

Lemon Pie he's coming through our commander still Space dog lines secure Space dog

Deck the halls I'm young again I'm you again racing turtles the grapefruit is winning seems I keep getting this story twisted so where's Neil when you need him deck the halls it's you again it's you again somewhere someone must know the ending is she still pissing in the river now heard she'd gone moved into a trailer park

so sure those girls now are in the Navy those bombs our friends can't even hurt you now and hold those tears cause they're still on your side don't hear the dogs barking don't say you know we've gone Andromeda stood with those girls before the hair in pairs it just got nasty and now those girls are gone

Space Dog

Words and Music by Tori Amos

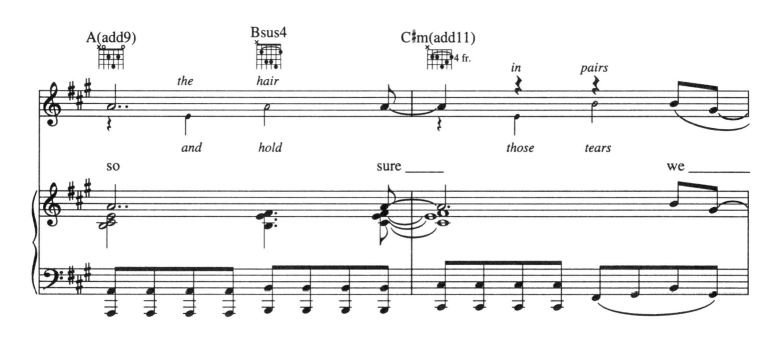

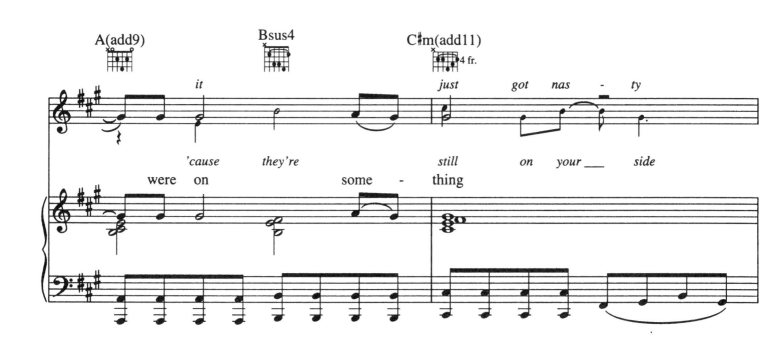

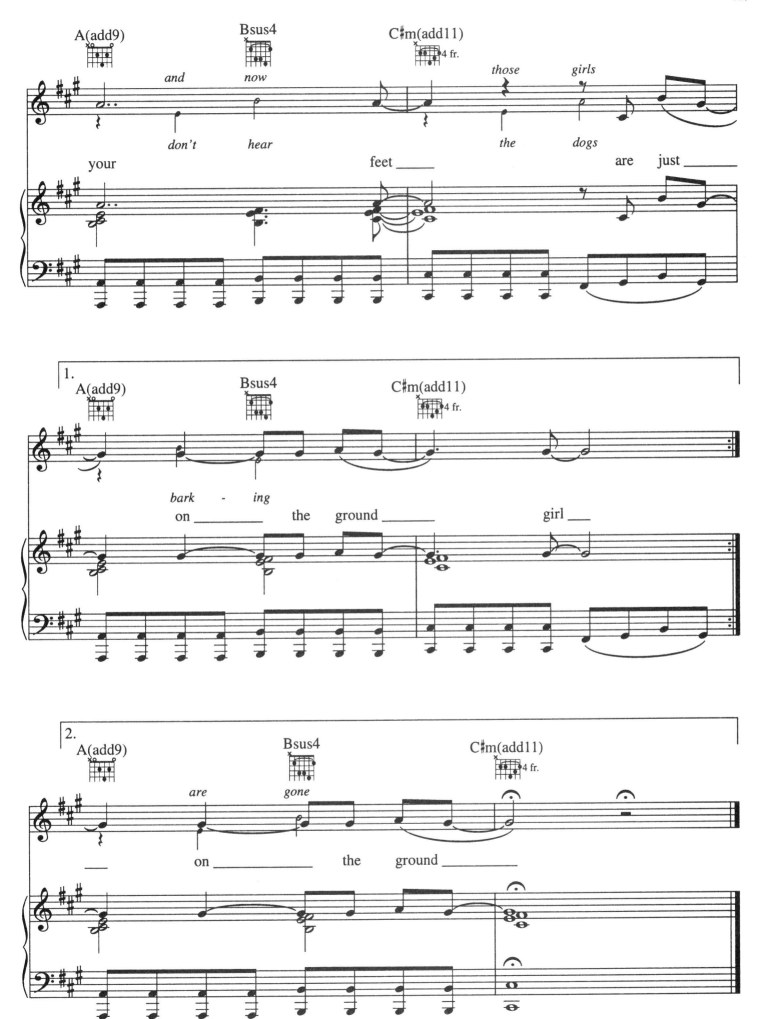

Baker Baker

Baker Baker baking a cake make me a day make me whole
again and I wonder
what's in a day what's in your cake this time

I guess you heard he's gone to L.A. he says that behind my
eyes I'm hiding and he
tells me I pushed him away that my hearts been hard to
find

here there must be something here there must be something
here here

Baker Baker can you explain if truly his heart was made of
icing and I wonder how
mine could taste maybe we could change his mind

I know you're late for your next parade you came to make
sure that I'm not
running well I ran from him in all kinds of ways guess it
was his turn this time

time thought I'd made friends with time thought we'd be
flying maybe not this time

Baker Baker baking a cake make me a day make me whole
again and I wonder if
he's ok if you see him say hi

Baker Baker

Words and Music by Tori Amos

Cornflake Girl

Never was a cornflake girl thought that was a good solution hangin with the raisin girls she's gone to the other side givin us a yo heave ho things are getting kind of gross and I go at sleepy time this is not really happening you bet your life it is

Peel out the watchword just peel out the watchword

She know what's goin on seems we got a cheaper feel now all the sweeteaze are gone gone to the other side with my encyclopedia they musta paid her a nice price she's puttin on her string bean love this is not really happening you bet your life it is

Rabbit where'd you put the keys girl and the man with the golden gun thinks he knows so much Rabbit where'd you put the keys girl

Cornflake Girl

Words and Music by Tori Amos

The Waitress

So I want to kill this waitress She's worked here a year longer than I If I did it fast you know that's an act of kindness

But I believe in peace I believe in peace Bitch I believe in peace

I want to kill this waitress I can't believe this violence in mind and is her power all in her club sandwich

I want to kill this killing wish they're too many stars and not enough sky Boys all think she's living kindness ask a fellow waitress ask a fellow waitress

The Waitress

Words and Music by Tori Amos

Slowly, in 2

Hey Jupiter

no one's picking up the phone
guess it's me and me
and this little masochist
she's ready to confess
all the things that I never thought
that she could feel and

hey Jupiter
nothings been the same
so are you gay
are you blue
thought we both could use a friend
to run to
and I thought you'd see with me
you wouldn't have to be something new
sometimes I breathe you in

and I know you know
and sometimes you take a swim
found your writing on my wall
if my hearts soaking wet
Boy your boots can leave a mess
hey Jupiter
nothings been the same
so are you gay

are you blue
thought we both could use a friend
to run to
and I thought I wouldn't have to keep
with you
hiding

thought I knew myself so well
all the dolls I had
took my leather off the shelf
your apocalypse was fab
for a girl who couldn't choose between
the shower or the bath

and I thought I wouldn't have to be
with you
a magazine

no one's picking up the phone
guess it's clear he's gone

and this little masochist
is lifting up her dress
guess I thought I could never feel
the things I feel
hey Jupiter

Hey Jupiter

Words and Music by Tori Amos

Caught a Lite Sneeze

Caught a lite sneeze caught a lite breeze
caught a lightweight lightningseed
boys on my left side
boys on my right side

boys in the middle
and you're not here I need a big loan
from the girl zone

building
tumbling down
didn't know our love was so small
couldn't stand at all
Mr St. John just bring your son

the spire is hot
and my cells can't feed
and you still got that Belle dragging your foots
I'm hiding it well Sister Ernestine
but I still got that Belle
dragging my foots

right on time you get closer
and closer
called my name but there's no way in
use that fame
rent your wife and kids today
maybe she will
maybe she will caught a lite sneeze
dreamed a little dream
made my own pretty hate machine
boys on my left side
boys on my right side
boys in the middle and you're not here
boys in their dresses
and you're not here
I need a big loan from the girl zone

Caught A Lite Sneeze

Words and Music by Tori Amos

Moderately slow, steady

* Tori plays this figure throughout – Ed.

Caught a lite__ sneeze__   caught a lite__ breeze____

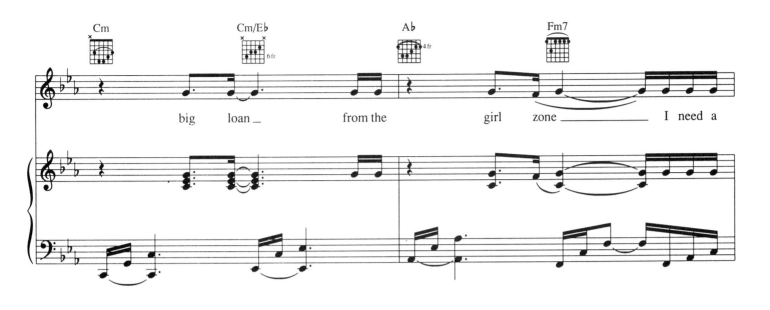

big loan ___ from the girl zone _____ I need a

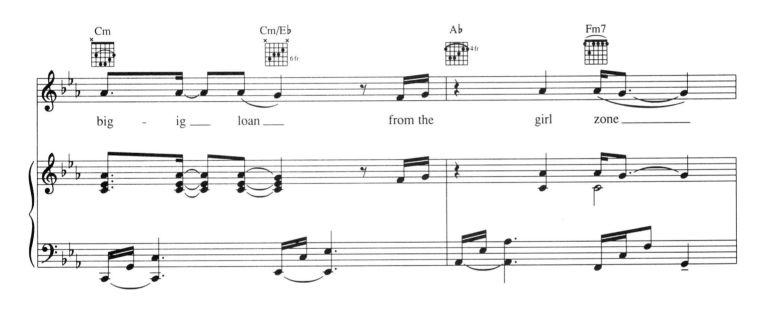

big - ig ___ loan ___ from the girl zone _____ I need a

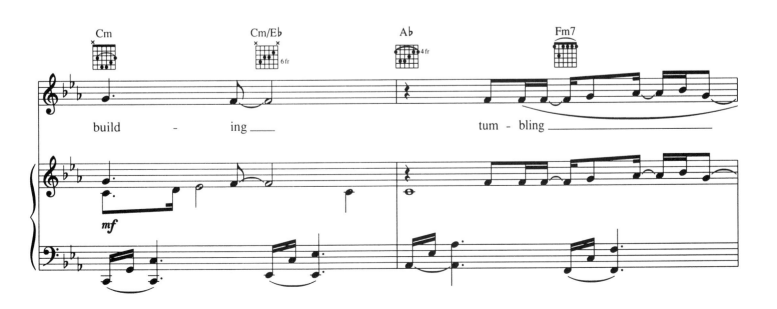

build - ing ___ tum - bling _____

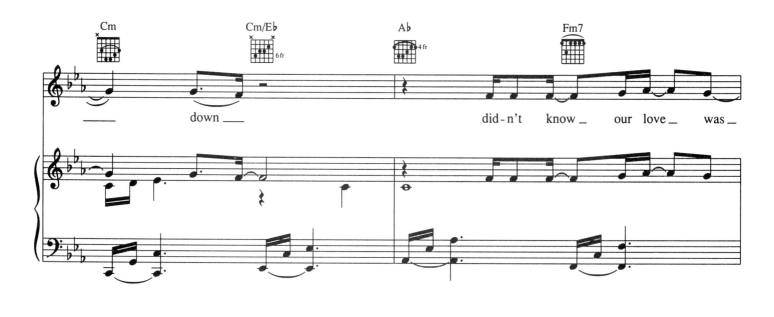

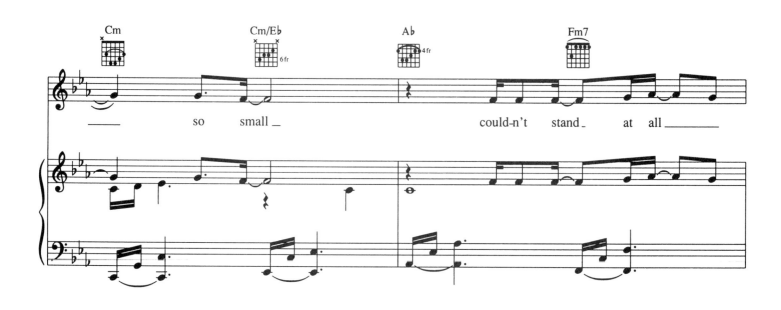

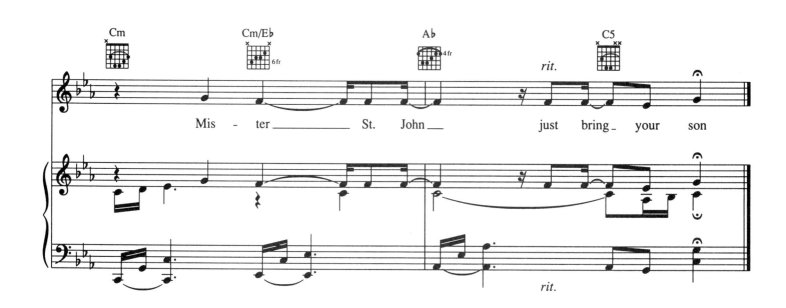

Father Lucifer

Father Lucifer
you never looked so sane
you always did prefer the drizzle to the rain
tell me that you're still in love with that Milkmaid
how's the Lizzies
how's your Jesus Christ been hanging

nothings gonna stop me from floating
nothings gonna stop me from floating

he says he reckons I'm a watercolour stain
he says I run and then I run from him
and then I run
he didn't see me watching
from the aeroplane
he wiped a tear
and then he threw away our appleseed

nothings gonna stop me from floating

everyday's my wedding day
though baby's still in his comatose state
I'll die my own Easter eggs
don't go yet
and Beenie lost the sunset but that's OK
does Joe bring flowers to Marilyn's grave
and girls that eat pizza and never gain weight
Father Lucifer you never looked so sane

Father Lucifer

Words and Music by Tori Amos

1.,3. Fath - er Lu - ci - fer___ you nev - er looked so sane
2. he says he reck - ons I'm___ a wat - er - col - our stain

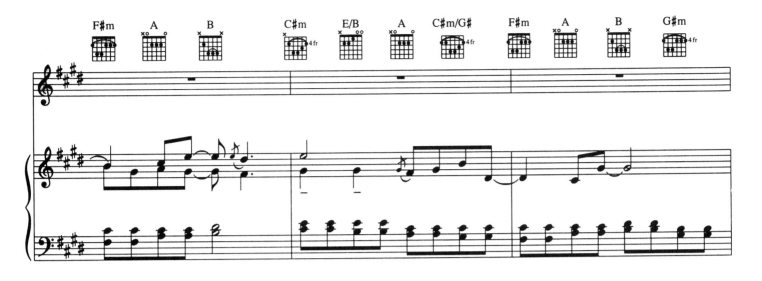

D.S. al Coda ⊕

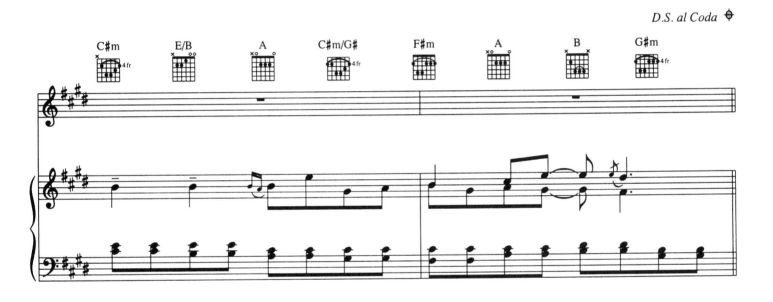

⊕ **Coda**

Putting The Damage On

glue
stuck to my shoes
does anyone know why you play with
an orange rind
you say you packed my things
and divided what was mine you're off to
the mountain top
I say her skinny legs could use sun
but now I'm wishing
for my best impression
of my best Angie Dickinson
but now I've got to worry
cause boy you still look pretty
when you're putting the damage on

don't make me scratch on your door
I never left you
for a Banjo

I only just turned around for a poodle
and a corvette
and my impression
of my best Angie Dickinson
but now I've got to worry
cause boy you still look pretty
when you're putting the damage on

I'm trying not to move
it's just your ghost
passing through
I said
I'm trying not to move
it's just your ghost passing through
it's just your ghost
passing through
and now
I'm quite sure
there's a light in your platoon
I never seen a light move
like yours
can do to me
so now I'm wishing
for my best impression
of my best Angie Dickinson
but now I've got to worry
cause boy you still look pretty
to me
but I've got a place to go
I've got a ticket to your late show
and now I'm worrying cause even still
you sure are pretty
when you're putting the damage on
yes
when you're putting the damage on
you're just so pretty
when you're putting the damage on

Putting The Damage On

Words and Music by Tori Amos

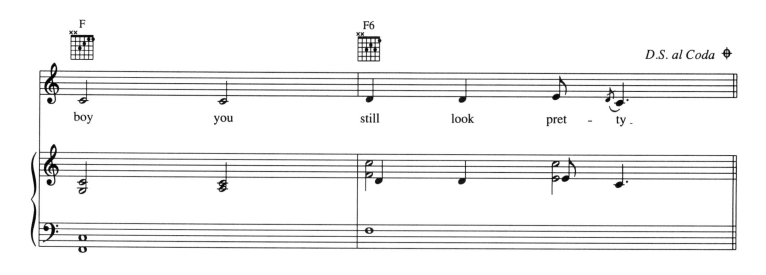

D.S. al Coda

boy   you   still   look   pret - ty

Coda

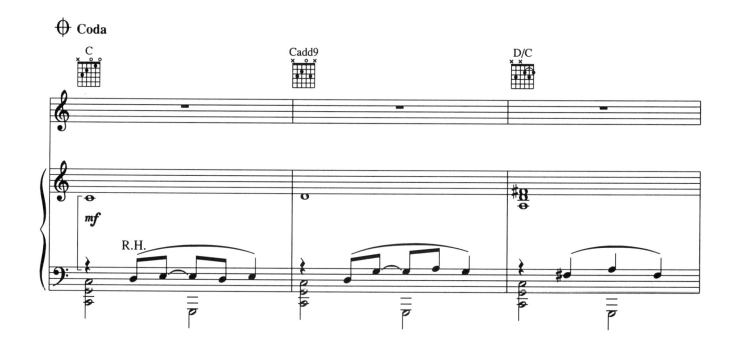

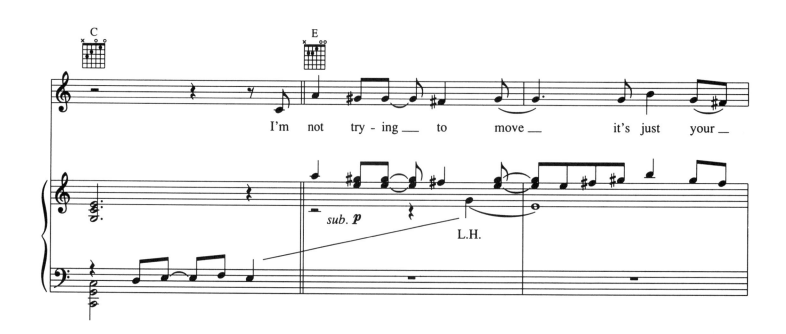

I'm   not   try - ing ___ to   move ___   it's just   your ___

Professional Widow

slag pit
stag shit
honey bring it close to my lips
yes
don't blow those brains yet
we gotta be big boy
we gotta be big
starfucker just like my Daddy
just like my Daddy selling his baby
just like my Daddy

gonna strike a deal make him feel
like a Congressman
it runs in the family
gonna strike a deal make him feel
like a Congressman
it runs in the family

rest your shoulders Peaches and Cream
everywhere a Judas as far as you can see
beautiful angel
calling "we got every re-run of Muhammad Ali"

prism perfect
honey bring it close to your lips
yes
what is termed a landslide of principle
proportion boy it gotta be big boy
starfucker just like my Daddy
just like my Daddy selling his baby
just like my Daddy
gonna strike a deal make him feel
like a Congressman
it runs in the family
Mother Mary
china white
brown may be sweeter

she will supply
Mother Mary
china white
brown may be sweeter
she will supply
she will supply
she will supply
she will supply

Professional Widow

Words and Music by Tori Amos

Northern Lad

Had a northern lad
well not exactly had
he moved like the sunset
god who painted that
first he loved my accent
how his knees could bend
I thought we'd be ok
me and my molasses
But I feel something is wrong
But I feel this cake just isn't done
Don't say that you Don't
and if you could see me now
said if you could see me now
girls you've got to know
when it's time to turn the page
when you're only wet
because of the rain

he don't show much these days
it gets so fucking cold
I loved his secret places
but I can't go anymore
"you change like sugar cane"
says my northern lad
I guess you go too far
when pianos try to be guitars
I feel the west in you
and I feel is falling apart too
Don't say that you Don't
and if you could see me now
said if you could see me now
girls you've got to know
when it's time to turn the page
when you're only wet
because of the rain
when you're only wet
because of the rain

Northern Lad

Words and Music by Tori Amos

Spark

she's addicted to nicotine patches
she's addicted to nicotine patches
she's afraid of the light in the dark
6.58 are you sure where my spark is
here
here
here
she's convinced she could hold back a glacier
but she couldn't keep Baby alive
doubting if there's a woman in there somewhere
here
you say you don't want it again
and again but you don't really mean it
you say you don't want it
this circus we're in
but you don't you don't really mean it you don't really mean it
if the Divine master plan is perfection
maybe next time I'll give Judas a try
trusting my soul to the ice cream assassin
here
you say you don't want it again
and again but you don't really mean it
you say you don't want it
this circus we're in
but you don't you don't really mean it you don't really mean it
how many fates turn around in the overtime
ballerinas
that have fins that you'll never find
you thought that you were the bomb yeah well so did I
say you don't want it
say you don't want it
say you don't want it again
and again but you don't really mean it
say you don't want it
this circus we're in
but you don't you don't really mean it you don't really mean it
she's addicted to nicotine patches
she's afraid of the light in the dark
6.58 are you sure where my spark is
here

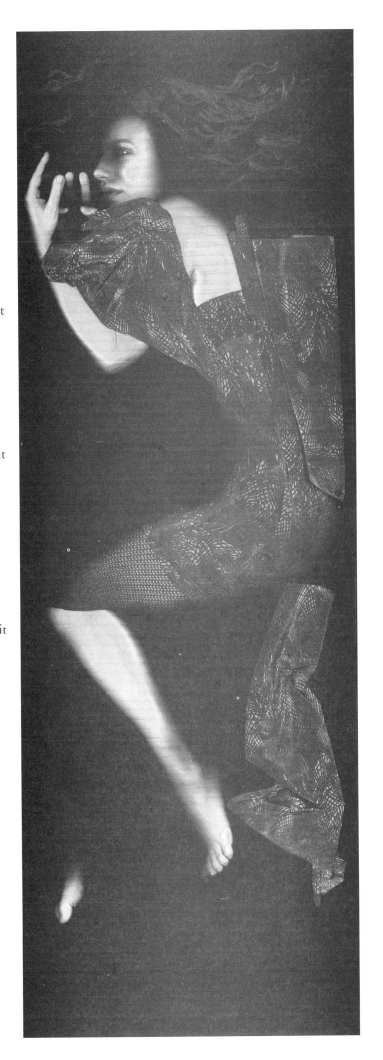

Spark

Words and Music by Tori Amos

she's ad- dict- ed to nic- o- tine patch- es